ravies pinx.

7ᵐᵉ Ordre
RUMINANTS

Chameau à une bosse ou D

VS *OS MARSUPIAUX* (Is. G. St Hil.)

adaire. (Camelus Dromedarius, *L.*) ¹/24 de grandeur natur.

POEMS

FOR

THE

CAMEL

JOHN BARRALE'S

POEMS FOR THE CAMEL

IS WINNER OF THE 2018

COSMOGRAPHIA CHAPBOOK PRIZE

The Cosmographia Chapbook Prize is
awarded annually to an exceptional chapbook
of transcendent poems. Contest ususally runs
September through January.

Learn more at CosmographiaBooks.com

To Linda

10/13/18

POEMS

FOR

THE

CAMEL

JOHN BARRALE

COSMOGRAPHIA

ROCHESTER, NY

[handwritten inscription on left margin:] thank you for loving me and ... ... Best regards, John

Book and cover design by Nina Alvarez

For permission to reprint portions of this book,
or to order a review copy, contact:
Editor@CosmographiaBooks.com

ISBN-13: 978-1-7322690-0-2
ISBN-10: 1-7322690-0-9

For Melina, Valentina, and Elise

P O E M S

For the Camel

And the blinking minotour is dragged from the dungeon

Of Ages Past and Present

Now Playing on the Home Box Office in Our House

For the Camel

"I didn't go to the moon. I went much further
 —for time is the longest distance between
two places."

—Tennessee Williams, *The Glass Menagerie*

BY THE BANKS OF THE NILE
(COMMENDS ON AN IMAGINED PAINTING)

I.

An 18th Century French explorer mesmerized Paris with his lectures on the Upper Nile. Each lecture ended with the story of an itinerant Arab peddler, who along with his wife, infant son, and their camel were killed by a pack of hyenas. As he told the story, the explorer would slowly unveil an enormous oil painting that depicted the event.

They are encircled. The peddler grips his musket by the barrel, wielding it like a club. A dead hyena lies at the peddler's feet. The peddler's dark, bearded face is imbued with courage. It is clear that he will fight to the death. The peddler's wife is young, thin, and tall, taller than he. She holds her baby over her head as a hyena jumps trying to take the infant. From her fierce expression, it is clear that she will also fight to the death. The camel's haunches are bloodied and torn. One of its legs is extended in a kick aimed at a lunging hyena.

The picture has many inaccuracies. The peddler wears bright yellow pantaloons, an embroidered tunic, and a red fez, attire suitable for the seraglio of a Mozart opera but not the bush. The woman's robe is teal-colored and clings too tightly, revealing the outline of her breasts. Her robe's color, and the fit of her bodice, would have been forbidden in that time and place.

Surprisingly, the center of the painting is the camel's
face. It looks directly at the viewer. The camel's neck is
arched, and its head is thrown back in a silent scream,
the moment forever frozen. That the family and camel
will die are only a part of the painting's meaning and
power.

II.

If I could erase the cruel moment
and save them—
I would,

for she to sit again
beneath the fragrant lemon tree
in her father's garden,

and there to give her breasts for suckle
to her son,

and he, the proud young father,
his face, the tawny dawn
of a beard's beginning,
would watch
and smoke his pipe
resting in the brown shade
of the mud-brick wall,

and the camel would chew his cud,
content in the labor of backyard fields
and the water wheel,

and as camels do,
would only bray
and kick
at the familiar
barking faces
of farm dogs.

Cape May, New Jersey: Memories of an Old House

Ah, but I talk too much for an old house.
Enough now. Understand the rest on your own.
Take the Saturday tour. Meet my friends.
Some are well cared for, others rundown.
But all, like me, are well past one hundred,
with the sun still hot, the rain still wet,
and the termites gnawing.

Yet, with brick and mortar souls,
we stand the watch like knights of old.

Oh, but how the nights tease us
when the stars rise
like lovers from their beds,
and comb the silver light
to let it fall in laughter
from their hair

while we look up,

John Barrale

our eyes aglow in varnish,
our smiles framed and stiff,
the green of summer wood
now forever stilled.

* * *

Our worth is of another day's—
its measure penny nails
and yards of wood,

the morning's beauty born of hammers,
their cawing noisy, iron birds
on scaffolds raw and climbing,

each new angle given lift
by a merry burst of song,

the midday sun vine-like ropes and veins,
the carpenter's sleeves rolled up
his strong arms set to working.

Poems for the Camel

But his whistling is over,
his day done,
his lunch pail forgotten
left to rust,

its red running like mice
under the porch.

Oh, but how the seasons fell,
oak and pine in one green chord
of perfect days.

How I miss their dog,
old and gentle
she bought the autumn in
on her paws.

* * *

Five blocks long, with ample trees,
we form a shaded line.
On windy days we clutch our roofs like hats,
and look out to the sea.

John Barrale

Our silence in perfect compliment
to the cries of the gulls
and the Cape's afternoon light.

SHAKESPEARE'S MOTHS

I. The Swarm

We fight in blinding, searing, arcs that cut like swords.
Our souls half insect, half man, angels slaved
to engines of ill design
that compel us to rise each night
in wild careening flights.
Our faith is the bomber's— beads and relics held in hand
as we circle in ships with masts like crosses.
Black sails, dark prayers—the words flags unfurled in war.
Who will be our God? Silent, furious, we ask,
our bodies beating against the flames,
until in singing ash we fall
to become the ground's cruel swordplay,
our limbs hacked and carried off by crawlers,
our wings their blood red trophies on their sill.

John Barrale

II. The Duel

Juliet! Juliet! I have fallen!
My love for you is sweeter than all the fields of France.
You are Eve's garden ripe and wild,
its rich life spilling over in colors that stain the ground.
The curve of your wanton hip shames a guileless god.
Your hands let flowers fall in colored petals
to a green, green, earth.
I dream of you as a saint.
Your grace transforms these words to birds,
then to children, then to stars.
My death is nothing now, a drug I take
that tastes of blood and dreams.
When I awake, I will stand on different shores—
 my sword raised against the sun.

III. The Raid on God's House

I saw Him once,
His house beneath me on the ancient road
that rose and canted in the light like a dream.
As I tapped, He peered through the glass,
an invalid blind as the stars.
His face was disdainful as a king's,
the eyes, though, were a beggar's—
vacant, and milked over. Common.
Brown, not blue. Divinity balding,
hidden under an old campaign hat,
He raised a trembling, veined hand
and with a shake of the curtain shooed me away.
Then without a word, as if I had never been born,
He turned His back.

John Barrale

IV. To Sleep, Perchance to Dream

Nineteen raids, twenty nights.
How I long for the end of summer's tapping!
Oh, to be a wriggler again, cocooned
and safe in the crystal bed of winter.
There to sleep, perchance to dream
the little dreams of shoots and leaves,
and, there again, to hear the old ones
humming in their wells,
and, there again, to watch them spin
their night sky myths
of a heaven careless and rich.
Eternity, calling like a window left open.
My God, my God, why are sins so fast
and wings so slow?

SPROUT

Childhood? My mother told me stories
about my grandfather
who was taken for a ship's timber—
cut down in a flail of sweating arms
and buzzing saws—
his stump left in the ground's mouth,
a half-pulled rotting tooth.

Mother mourned for more than thirty rings of growth,
told me she often saw transmissions in her branches—
pictures unimaginable of water vaster than any lake
and a sun that rose fiery at dawn,
its face unpleasant, skull-like
and too hot — a real grass scorcher,
except there was no grass.

Of my father, I remember little.
He was taken while I was still a sprout.
My mother says for planks. What kind?
As the saying goes, she leaves those knots

John Barrale

in the branch for me to fill.

I'd like to think he ended up wild, a circus wagon
hauling something big, and red, and noisy.
My brother, who knew him, says no,
probably just plain, old flooring.

Europa

Her curly hair, now pine and oak forests,
has a rosy glow in the morning light.
And those cliffs under her eyes, weary
and like violet half-moons,
are still adorably mortal.

Mussed, her shores are livid after storms.
But always a high-born, she welcomes the men
who paint their faces blue.
Men who bump their pea-pod boats
against her sides, and wrap garlands
around her mighty oaks
while she marvels at how those trees
just yesterday were sprouts.

Later, much later, after Gaul
and Hun and Roman bang their swords,
saints will claim her. She'll hardly care.
She was giant, so much more than a man-god,

John Barrale

a millennium before their Christ was born.
Red wine flowed in veins then
stronger than any blood.
And gods had horns and balls,
were apt to take a fancy to a pretty woman.

History is something she hates.
No past. No present. No future—
time just a jumble of tenses,
like the boulders,
at the foot of her alps.

But sometimes, changing back to a woman,
darkly-darkly she will go
padding through the night.

And coming to a glen, she will let her sorrow go—

give it wing, and breath, and let it find its voice
in the sharp cry and snap of a mouse
taken by an owl.

In my re-imagining of the myth, Zeus changes Europa into the continent of Europe.

Lady Moon Remembers
and Mourns   5 Songs—

I.

Somewhere, deep in time's memory,
the moon still swirls
over malignant swamps
    and choke forests
    of fern

where giant birds of prey screech
and beasts now extinct quicken
rising again at dusk to hunt—

the lame
and the slow
caught
    and by fierce jaws
taken up.

The air gray, always gray,

the time before Eden,
mostly fog
and rain,

every night rain,
     rain
before dawn.

2.

Much later, there are ships. Adventure.

To see them is like seeing once more
the beginning of the world.

Hearts, young hearts,
     like sea flowers,
blossom,
     seek glory.

Jason steals the Golden Fleece.

Troy falls, a mighty roaring hymn

that breaks her heart,
and Ulysses
sails beyond the Gates of Hercules
a moonstone for luck
   sewn in his cloak.

3.

Lady moon remembers the names
   of the Scottish kings
   who gave her
their captives'
heads,

and the swoop and fell
of the highlands she guarded

where crones
   with broken teeth
and wild bracken hair
in secret
sang moon prayers.

She gorges,
    swallows again every detail,
every spear raised in triumph,
every dog tribe
and wolf pack's
howl.

She was magic, the stick
    and stone shrine
in the glen,
    and the circle of pebbles
in front of the hut.

Witches danced to her moods,
and silken-haired maids
prayed their first cycle came in her fullness,
    her light cast like a spell
on the fields where they lay,

a leering assurance of husbands
    and fertile wombs.

4.

Lady moon, now a Pop icon
     and a Rock Star,
still accepts the thanks of lovers,
     and the moon-light inspired chirps
of crickets—
enchanting creatures, her favorites;

     something she would paint
upon a lacquered fan
     if she could.

5.

Lady Moon wants to be
     the dun-colored continent
she was
before being torn from her mother,
     the earth.

Bird-like beasts loped into flight
     from her plains

and caught fish
skimming her lakes,
their enormous leathery wings
    opening like sails.

She hears their cries in the wind,
remembers what was lost
    when she sees a gull fly.

How sad, she thinks,
    to never feel the rain,
and watch ships pass,

ships with sails once new and tan
before the sun, and time
    bleached
their color.

Only with age do sails
    and gulls
    and moons
turn white.

Now, resigned, she illuminates the small.

A poet, she loves to touch a tree's branches,
    make whisper the shapes of stones,
and cast shadows on the lines jungle ants make
    when by her light they travel.

Tonight she feels thin and lonely, dim
against the brightness of the cities.

    Like a giant hand,
she hangs from the sky's sleeve,
her fingers
    opening and closing.

So I begin. So I end,
she thinks.

    And who but God
could cut my claws,
    and only then,
with the edge of the sun.

THE RAIN RUNNERS
- *FOR THE HOMINIDS*

The rain strokes the dirt, and the wet smell attracts me. Under my feet,

the bones of my ancestors circle and smile coiling like friendly snakes.

Their secret graves are everywhere, and they want to talk if only I listen.

I imagine their faces, and make up stories the lonely me wants to hear:

that one, ten-thousand generations ago, fathered a tribe.

Though he and his children had no language, they knew colors

and gathered berries. The one over there took care of her teeth.

I can see the twigs she used to brush them.

That one, standing shyly in the corner, was too proud

and starved. The sad one, tugging his forelock,

had a wife he loved, but she was taken by a lion.

Were they, like me, afraid? Or, were they brave

when storms came, daring the thunder

to run in the rain?

Their lives once filled with birdsong are now ash,

the outline of what was almost invisible,

and as free as the salt that rises from the sea

and falls with the rain—

nothing at all like their capricious smiles

and whirling minds

when their lives were like mine

above the ground.

And the blinking minotaur

is dragged from the dungeon

THE FOURTEEN

Tied back to back they wait,
their faces dulled and somber
like the shells of turtles.

Then the command
and the sudden rough pull
of the ropes,

ten men struggling

and the blinking Minotaur is dragged
from the dungeon,

its horns
wildly thrusting,

the naked body swaying,
and shameless
in its lust.

John Barrale

Their bonds cut,
they are told to enter.

To run is useless, yet they try
holding each other's hands
at the start.

Soon it is over, the darkness
opening its mouth,
Daedalus' maze,
like a cheap backdrop,
shaking.

* *To atone for the death of Androgeus, the son of Crete's King Minos, the Athenians sent seven maidens and seven youths to Crete every nine years. There, they were given to the Minotaur a monster who had the head of a bull and the body of a man, who killed and devoured them. Eventually, Theseus, one of the youths sent to Crete, killed the Minotaur.*

But, that is another story.

ABOUT THE STOVE

The cruel stove that burned the pots will be in ruins.
Scraps of egg from breakfast crucifixions will litter its top.
The ghosts of gladiator mice will fight
to their third and fourth deaths.
Emperor cats as lean as crescent moons
will watch and wait
to eat the winners.
And within the burner's rusting rings
the Saints of fire will slow dance one last time
their glorious boogalo growing ever smaller
in simmering circles of derelict gas,
until each disappears like a pretty woman
into the lonely black lens
of the Orbison pilot light.

DEAD TOES

Gleeful in their rot, the toes break off
and like ten drunk monks
go their separate ways.

Their huts will crumble,
sides and roofs
never to be trimmed again,
clipped,
or painted.

The government that regulated such things
is no longer in charge—
the distant King or Queen
has abdicated,
their clicking scissor parliaments
and brass trimmer police
are silent, shut up
and forgotten
in cabinet,

pocket,

or purse.

Some toenails, the hard-core anarchists,

refuse to die, and flare up

in an after-death revolution.

Defiant, they grow unchecked

for a few more grisly weeks,

their edges curling hideously.

It doesn't matter—

the motion factory is abandoned,

the foot's parts on strike,

arch, heel, and instep

siding with the seven sisters

called the Tarsals

and leaving the ankle.

Too late, the folly!

Hell is hot!

John Barrale

The workhorse foot muscles
aren't there to pull them back
like in better times
when the toes were young
and the water was too cold,
or the sand too hot.

The Buddha Big Toe
warned of this—

We are nothing, an illusion,
ten small ghosts gliding
in a dream of motion.

The Eye After Death

Bones remain, not the eye:
its parts too soft,
the aqueous humor,
the iris and cornea,
the watery liquid,
and the thick jelly
are soon dissolved.

The images of a lifetime,
freed of obligations,
go nowhere.

One hour after,
the eye's teacup ocean
is windless.

By cruel design,
it fills with aimless,
drifting things.

John Barrale

Slowly they sink.

Sailors and passengers abandon ship.

The optic nerve,
once so vibrant,
stops telegraphing images.

Silent, it lies in a place without light,
a cold stone in a tomb
where all gods are refused,
and no image forms itself
from a spark.

Death for the blind is different.

Their dead eyes open
and begin to see.

Forest Voices

I flinch from the sparks.

Everything is blurs and ashes.
Once in a while, a cloud separates
and breaks from the herd
crowding the sky above me.
This lets a star,
like a brilliant mistake,
break through.

* * *

Night is a buzzing flail.

The moon's rising
makes the raccoons drunk.

The smell of wet fur

John Barrale

from mating skunks
is a cold, sharp odor.
Mushrooms, like blossoms
from another world,
fill in my cracks
and crevices.

Everything around me
feeds in the night
and sleeps in the day.

* * *

The seasonal melodies of the geese have ended.
The wind plaits straw grass into ugly hats.

Like a predictable bout of insanity,
the snow begins.

* * *

I have lived through a string
of dry, thirsty weeks.

The rain is such an amazing,
hysterical thing!

* * *

Put down roots.
Speak only with green lips.
Listen with wooden ears
then pretend you're deaf.
Cover your heart with bark.
Your sap is a secret.
Keep safe your twigs.
Pruning is not an option.

Of Ages Past

and Present

Suzhou, China

Suzhou, I am brought to your heart
like a cricket to market,
my small wildness riding
in a painted bamboo cage,
and tied to you by silk threads.

My chirping is shushed
by the beauty of your gardens
and the humpbacked bridges
that open like paper fans
over your canals.

Suzhou, phantom lovers
slip along your terracotta walls.
They glide in moonlight
over the barges,
and the spread of a woman's hair
as she bathes in the river.

John Barrale

In the mountains it rains.
The lake in autumn is flooded.

Suzhou, when will I be home?

✳   ✳   ✳

At nightfall, swans gather
alongside the bridge.
They arch their necks
and coyly sway.
Our guide tells the story
of a Wu emperor's wife
who met her lover
in the shadows
along the riverbank.

I am saddened.
The bridges connect nothing now.

The summer palaces are abandoned.
Robed in vines, they stand in silence,
old men without memory.

* * *

And what of the emperor's wife and her lover?

She was put to death.
But, as legend tells, first blinded
and made to walk in robes of shame
through Suzhou's gardens.

Of him, nothing is remembered.

But of their lives,
a few museum pieces remain:
her jade hairpin,
his ink stone,
and a bronze cricket,
its small perfection the favorite toy
of an emperor's bastard son.

Saint Anne de Beaupre

Poem 1

Was there a golden age before words
when prayers exactly matched
the howling of the soul?
(A time when time had no seams
and height was up, and depth down,
when we could crane our necks
and see heaven's walls,
and our faces
mirrored in the sunlit wings
of angels—
just that lost and perfect moment,
cloudless and clear,
of looking up,
before we, in an instant,
lived out our lives,
and, while the angel blinked,
fell down,

grew old,
withered
and died)

Poem 2

In old Jerusalem, there is an alley
where you can rent love by the hour,
where you can kiss a stranger's mouth
until, lost in sweetness like a burrowing insect,
you climb inside
while the air beats like wings
in waves of heat,
and fills with angels
heavy as stone.

Was it like this for you, Anne?

Or were you frightened when the angel spoke
and you were caught,
your thighs wet
and half broken
like a fish in an eagle's beak.

John Barrale

Poem 3

Yesterday it rained in Quebec. The wind was thin, all flutes and pipes.

It carried the smell of methane. This morning the sky was dark,

and came in low, made me think of storms,

and how the city would look in the snow.

History flares here in capes and tri-cornered hats.

Cartier and Champlain sailed down this river.

Jacques thought the quartz on the cliffs were diamonds

and called the rock on which Quebec is built Cap Diamant.

Samuel settled here, later gave his name to a lake.

Don't look for the half-naked, whinnying wives

of the warriors who watched. Gone.

River goddesses now, they sleep with the drowned.

The Citadel's ruins light up at 5:00 like a café.

Across, on the Plains of Abraham, old cannon stare.

Freshly painted, and with open mouths,

they look like bored waiters.

Montcalm and Wolfe waltzed here.

Blood bouquets blossomed on their shirts.

Soldier ghosts in leggings snap to, and in the square

the souls of the converted tribes kneel in unison

when the bells ring three times and the Host is raised.

Time makes fools of heroes. The brightest sabers rust.
Only you, Anne, have not scarred and pitted.
Who you were is safe, intact and cased,
your heart become the saint in the statue's plaster,
the struts and wires hidden,
known only to the artist.

Poem 4

Anne, the centuries pass like seasons along the St. Lawrence.

In spring, you traveled on the backs of the soldiers
while they cursed the mud and the arrows
that pinned them to the trees.

In summer the black-robe priest made you pretty,
a smiling grandmother in the children's picture book.

In autumn, you were a queen, the sunflower shedding her seeds.
You watched over the fields and sheltered the deer.

John Barrale

When fever came, you cradled a dying boy
holding him to your chest like a broken bird.

Come winter, the village girls made you a wreath.
Sensing death, the old and the sick lit candles.
One solemn frozen morning, ten strong men
lifted the tree that fell in front of your church.

Poem 5

Anne, come walk with me along the river.
Branches poke through the melting snow.
It's Spring. Words doze in the sun. Winter is forgiven.
Only you remember the old man and his daughter taken by the flu.
Does you house still have a beautiful room, a warm bed,
and a meal for the drunk the priest found frozen on the steps?

The brown grasses preach resurrection,
a lesson rising up they quiver
covered by new growth, raw, and not yet all green,
like the newly learned French Hail Marys
and Latin Our Fathers, burgeoning bits of grace

sticky on the lips of the Algonquian children.

Anne, can you still hear their ghosts recite the catechism.

Notes:

Anne was Christ's grandmother. Childless, after twenty years of marriage to Joachim, she gave birth to Mary.

St. Anne, the patron Saint of Quebec, is also the patroness of single women, women in labor, grandmothers, miners, and the M'kmaq people of Canada.

St Anne became the patroness of miners in the medieval ages when a connection was made between the Virgin Mary, Christ, and silver and gold. Anne's womb was considered the source from which these metals were mined. St Anne is also the patron saint of sailors, and a protector from storms.

"I beg you, holy mother Anne, send me a good and loving man." – *a popular 16th Century French peasant's prayer.*

Tutankhamen

-remembering The Boy King exhibit at the
NY Metropolitan Museum of Art

Yes. He lived a long time ago,
I answer—
my six-year-old's questions endless,
the afternoon tiring
spent on long lines
as we walk past the jewels,
the coins,
his crown.

Only what death has left is here—

the rings small enough
for a boy's finger,

the toy war chariot
pulled by jeweled horses,

the miniature servants
lined up in rows
by the clay urns,

and the scale in the corner
made of gold
so thin

it could only have weighed
the butterfly image of a soul
etched into its side.

A piece of his tomb's wall was taken,
lifted from the dark,
and now rests
with him,

a world scaled down,

the stonework scored
and filled,
complex, uneasy,
almost a living thing.

John Barrale

The hieroglyphics
and stick-figure gods
like dark flowers
blossom.

I would put
their petaled claws
in my mouth,

chew their clicks

and with my spit
give them life.

And in this communion,
I would feel his gods stir
and quicken,

their stars no longer fixed
but circling,

his time opening again

the lost faces
given flesh.

Someone behind me whispers,
  Look at the two jackal-headed figures.

Heavy-lidded
and blind,
set deep in the stone,
they are paired gods,
twin sisters,
Sleep and Death.

If only, I could rest.

*　*　*

Stubborn, I cling—
as night does to stars,
    as did the hands
that placed the mask
of gold
over his face
    and with tears

closed time's iron gate.

*   *   *

Do not mourn—
        I am the journey,
the soul's whisper,

the laughing boy
        who chased pigeons
along the tomb's
long length
of stone.

I will wake
        and smell the air
still sweet with myrrh.

My hands will find the place
        where my name is written,
and I will say the spells.

Light will sing my name!

Poems for the Camel

In a reed boat,
  I will cross the three rivers,
and go again to Thebes

MELVILLE

I am her vessel. She hovers on my lips.
An old hymn. A song of darkness. The book I am.
Am I singing her name out loud?
I am old and often can't remember
whether I am awake or dreaming.

Cocky, a young man, the sun behind me,
and all the world's water racing beneath me,
I thought I could make her my mistress.
Truth is, I didn't know the exchange,
what I would give and what she would take.

Now, I am wracked with pain, an old sea wreck.
Just look at my hands, twisted and broken.
She had her moods. I learned them fast.

They say she has no soul. Bullshit! She's one huge soul.
She breathes and lives. Old, yes, and frightening,
God's daughter's own hands in the storm's swell.

Forever my lover, she mastered me long ago
when, from boyhood shores, I watched her naked beauty,
her every heaving, violent wave a rape.

Damn you, and all, who would have me die in this bed.
If I could, I'd drown, take comfort from her rough hands
as she blurs the land from my face.
Gladly, I'd let her restless fingers polish me,
and her mouth suck the meat from my bones,
until like the whale's fierce jaw,
I am scoured, become scrimshaw,
something rich and strange.

Tintype of Men and a Boy Drinking and Smoking Cigars

Cigars and liquor stirred the conversation.

Those worth hearing paused before making their point.
Some stared into their glass as if the amber liquid
held the truth. Others stopped to examine their cigar
rolling it in practiced fingers before bringing it to mouth
where it was slowly puffed and a dot of red
coaxed out of the end.

A few, though, talked with what I would come to recognize
as the harrumph of good fellows back-slapping,
their words self-congratulating,
and thrown up into the air in flourishes
like a stage-actor waving a cane.

I was seventeen and new to the company of men,
so I said little, only answering when asked.

Poems for the Camel

Uncle Elias surprised me, poured me bourbon, the first I ever had,

the heavy crystal tumbler I drank from, a nine-weight,

shook in my hand.

My father gave me a cigar and ceremoniously lit it

with a scratch-tip match. The smoke was sweet

and not at all bitter like I thought it would be.

Though I had only smoked hand-rolled and corn silks,

I managed not to choke.

The smoke streamed from my nose

and felt hot along my lip.

I watched it rise to the porch's ceiling

where it broke against the beams and vanished.

When I looked about, I realized I was alone.

Everyone had gone into the house.

St. Bonaventure's—

GRAVEYARD AND CHAPEL

The headstones are weathered, some scoured down
to almost nothing, the names
of the dead erased,
and like the ships
they berthed
forgotten—
hulls and men slipping under,
rogue and hero
made immaculate again,
this time slowly,
this time
by the land's
wind
and rain.

*   *   *

My grave is plain. No statue in miracle
whispers my name,

nor child or widow
come to grieve
and light a candle.

The steeple's bells can't ring,
their tongues in 1812 were pulled—
taken for cannon and anchor,

and now the priest
sends a boy running
to call the girls in the village
to their weddings.

The faithful, bell-less
and Sunday-morning deaf,
seldom trudge up the hill.

I laugh— my ghost,
all shadows and dust,
frightens no one.
I am a relic, without use
like Bonaventure's bones
buried beneath the altar. Forgotten—

John Barrale

I am among the many,
a lowly sailor,
taken by the sea.

*   *   *

One name, one name, each wave calls.

If you are young, your heart will yearn,
and every ship will be your father's spear,
every shore you leave
your mother's tears.

Go without care. Run to the sea.
Serve her well.

And when you are old,
you will hear her good wife's voice,
and touch again her shoulders,
remembering summer's fair weather
she wore like a dress.

*   *   *

The drowned will rise, their ships
made magnificent again.

On that day, you will hear their sails fill,
and smell the brine carried by the wind.

If you call out, they will not stop.

God speed, you think,
but can't say the words—
you, forever on the shore,
you who never left.

Long after that day, you'll remember their churning wake,
their gleaming bows, and white sails,
and how the waves were dark
and green,

and how when the last ship passed,
the setting sun fired
and sank into the sea.

AFTER THE LONG SIGH OF THE VIOLINS WOUND YOU BEYOND REPAIR

After the long sigh of the violins wound you beyond repair—

over beers with God, you look down and see how all is really small and ugly. God, reading your mind, says *I'm thinking bugs sucked dry and left hanging in a web.* You think of the mummified mouse you once found behind the boiler, a thing so ugly that even the old janitor in your head wouldn't get the broom and dustpan to pick it up.

After the long sigh of the violins wound you beyond repair—

you have the dream of deer and buttons. A buck, you'll be shot, strung up by a hunter, and slit from the neck down. One brown eye will harden into a button. Too small, it doesn't close your wounds. The nimble-fingered monkeys, who were the world's tailors back then, buy the idea and make it work. You become rich from the royalties, and all is good until 1895 when a lazy cat invents the zipper. Over pipes in God's favorite opium den, you complain. God tells you to write a book about how the animals invented everything. You wake up and think of the buttons on her blouse, closed shutters now.

After the long sigh of the violins wound you beyond repair—

you come back as your grandfather's grandfather. You'll live to be very old and survive three wives. Only an occasional dog will come scratching at your door. You'll remark to anyone who'll listen that you prefer your house to anything in the world, and you love the flowers in your garden better than your daughters. No one will really care. It won't matter because at night, in your bed, you'll hear the clock in the hall strike one, and see the future waiting like a long army encamped on the mountaintop your pillow makes.

After the long sigh of the violins wound you beyond repair—

memories melt faster than ice in bright sunlight. I remember January, you and our sons, the smiles frozen in the photograph. Somewhere there is snow on the ground, and silence grows to the size and weight of a house. My hands write furiously and make do with the warmth of a cup. Notions are altered, and hours that never counted open in petals. My fingers rise and bring forgotten touches up to my lips where they are rubbed and blessed.

7 Days Without Dates

I

In winter I skate ponds, my mind on the small places left over from summer's lakes. Edges are now set, the blurred shapes frozen into images, my thought trapped like a frog in the ice. All the small things that inhabit the heart have been put away, the lines of memory at the bottom, water's etchings seen through ice.

II

Foolish me, how I linger beyond my time and place. Each moment now doomed to blaze, a funeral ship in fire's grace. I watch you sleep. The long legs of dreams run across your face. Logs in the woodstove mourn with me, sister ships they burn and settle down. If death be a desert, then, we, my love are the memory of rivers.

III

I am defenseless, a rabbit skin nailed to the crosspiece of a barn door, a small lesson of yard and fences, a piece of darkness to cover the coming winter brilliance, just enough for a child's glove.

IV

Last night it rained. This morning the eyes widen to take in hills opening like books on a giant table. Cattle fill the foreground. Horned heads are shards poking up from ruins. All the fields today are tired, their warriors no longer spinning.

V

The trees that gorged on color are now repentant. They pool their pain and give it back, vomiting leaves. Their branches wave, like arms signaling. One branch scrapes against the window.

VI

Wild geese pick through the fields, I startle them and they run to flight. Their feet pound the ground like blunt, blind pens smashing paper. But once in the air, they sky write perfectly. Their wings form words that only the ducks can read. Far below, cut corn lies scattered, dots and commas left behind, the fields below forgiven their fences.

VII

A jack-knifed trailer blocks the way. A tow truck tries to right it. So much is accident. Color drips from the leaves, comment, asides and irrational footnotes to the afternoon's unwritten poems. Insects zoom and swirl, so much freer than me. Which way is home? What compass points to long ago? I have no illusions left. Eden is where the leper boats go.

WHEN IT RAINS

When it rains

intersections are troubling. Familiar streets confuse, no matter how many times they've been crossed. Pedestrians huddle like lost sheep on the corners. The trouble is that many are wearing trench coats and look like detectives. But, unlike the movies, missing persons are never found on rainy nights.

When it rains

couples shelter in doorways and kiss. (The movies again). You can tell which are new lovers, their raincoats match. Dry people watch from behind windows. Blurred, their faces resemble the deep sea divers that a child places at the bottom of an aquarium and soon forgets.

When it rains

puddles form, the neighborhood's clumped refuse damming the runoff and filling the street's craters with new, shimmering constellations. Truck wheels return the water to the air. Headlights illuminate the faces waiting at a bus stop. Armored in coat and hat, and some holding umbrellas, they are indifferent to the splashes, each in their moment become the morning's first angel wet with grace and witness to creation.

When it rains

the streets are bathed in Sheba light, and my thoughts ride donkeys. I am cloaked, a gift, all imperfection hidden, a veiled bride promised to the night and taking new jeweled shape as she bends to gather the fractured light from glass and puddles. Only the traffic lights, like mountain brigands, dare to challenge my procession.

When it rains

each raindrop is a small comet sent from God. Streets that were safe, dusty places free their inner kingdoms and become dangerous. All pretense is washed away, the avenues in the glittering downpour becoming magnificent jezebels. St. Patrick's, wet and seething, its spires a nest of snakes, shouts out proclaiming its false brilliance in angry, marble songs.

When it rains

storm clouds lower darkening the river. Revolution is in the tense air. Lights from the tallest skyscrapers illuminate the others. And now the sky is battle, each building a soldier in the charging skyline. Architecture demands valor. Royalty is targeted, marked by its height. Who will win? Only the gargoyles know. Sharp-faced secret assassins with stone stilettoes, they wait to pounce.

When it rains

do not fear. You will rust slowly. The city with its brick fathers and iron mothers birthed you. Highway uncles and parkway aunts tried to take you away, but you stayed.

Now Playing on

the Home Box Office

in our House

HER CAT IN THE WINDOW
BLUE WITH RAIN

I remember
her cat
in the window
blue
with rain,

and slow April mornings,

the pages
of her
favorite books
turning
on the table,

breakfast scant

like her robe
printed
with flowers,

the taste of cigarettes,
and black coffee
sharp,

the sugar brown
and stirred in
with a white
plastic spoon.

I remember
her legs
dangling
over the edge
of the bed,

and the small
whisker sound
of nylons
pulled off
and on,

and the shyness
when she showed me

the broken china
she collected
and kept
in a box.

I remember
making love
on her
November-colored
rug,

her lace
and oyster
taste,

and the moon
coming through
the window

with its light

pale
on her belly.

John Barrale

I remember
Rue St. Denis
in December
covered in ice
and snow,

and the café
like a shiny miracle

open

at the bottom
of the hill,

the thin stems
of the wine glasses
twirling,

the bottles of wine
lined up in rows
so formal
and French.

I remember
her happy face
sitting across from me

and the bowl
of onion soup
we shared,

she closing
around
her pleasure
like the petals
of a flower,

she simple,
and there,

her face like her life,
creased with dreams.

Fifty years later and old dogs
loose in the heart
still sniff

John Barrale

at memory.

I wonder

does she ever think
of me?

HANDS

I look down at them
play God—
reduce the world's species to two

a left
&
a right,

my first act of non-creation
to downsize,
deconstruct,

decree
that there be

no beasts, no people,

no flowers,
no clouds

John Barrale

just fingers
and thumbs

because even God
needs angels.

& maybe
tomorrow,

when time
is scheduled to begin,

I'll let one
open the day
like a curtain.

A Few Good Sins

The master bedroom's high-ceilinged lights
often burn out, sending me down
to the basement for a ladder, a task
worth five Hail Marys
and six Our Fathers.
The toilet runs on
no matter how many times
I fidget with is guts. By the rules,
each half-hour, spent kneeling
and wet-fingered,
earns me equal time off
from purgatory's fires.
Scrubbing the tub, something I hate,
tips the golden scale in my favor
making up for several, truly, mortal sins.
The back door sticks when it rains,
and the kitchen cabinets
go bump in the night;
I suppose to remind me

the devil is hungry.
Unlike the path leading to Heaven's gate,
my front yard is clogged
with all the world's leaves.
Rake! Rake! Your soul depends on it!
Like a few good sins, summer blazes
through the missing pane
in the basement window.
Bugs and light slowly seep in
spreading up into the house.
I like this and won't fix it.

GRANDPARENTS

Nothing grows on top of their graves.

I won't allow it—
enjoying too much
when their legs break through
searching for the moon's face
like bone swords.

They often wake me
and gently perform rituals
of suffocation—
covering my nose and ears,
and the holes
in my heart.

They try to sing.
I suppose to please me—
happy songs from sad operas.

John Barrale

But they can't hold the long notes,
their chests, for the most part,
being empty.

Sometimes, they just sit on my bed
trying to scare me
with their 150 year old faces.

But I won't budge,
refusing to sign their death certificates.

Come back, I say
tomorrow night.

STILL LIFE

My thoughts are sated and fat,
and sit flush like guests who refuse to leave.
The words I write are crumbs
shaken off the tablecloth in boredom
while Bella, your lovebird, dances
on the edge of my notebook.
She, my pen, and your brushes
are now our children.
The warm sea-green of her feathers,
and the brown of the spilled coffee
rounding the saucer's white rim
mixes with the sun's butter yellow
and the kitchen red
bleeding like a heart.
Silence grows between us in spasms—
the warm feral colors coming and going,
a still life waiting for your brushes
that soak in a glass by the sink.

Morning Bucolic

Dawn is two blocks down
crossing the street.
I am hungry
and the morning opens
like a diner for breakfast—
the world's cream and sugar
stirred by your eyes.
Now I'm seeing it again,
inhaling the steam of summer
from the honky-tonk mugs,
the ones you bought last year
when we were in San Francisco.

ON A STREET IN KALISPELL

We could have gone on that way forever.

And in a way we did, slipping beyond time.

All the parts of us there and not there, playing on,

a movie they forgot to stop after the theater emptied.

You and I my love. On a street in Kalispell, Montana.

The Rockies are behind us now, on the American side,

waiting for the morning like a sleeping castle.

The new day is in our hands,

a paper-wrapped doughnut

and a cup of coffee,

the act of being you and I simple again,

just a shoelace we tie and untie in the half-light.

You and I my love. There and not there.

A presence unseen but felt.

Stars and planets in the daytime sky.

Home From Alaska

Last night, we ate fish.

I bit into a fried back
and thought of how like a thousand bee stings
the rough suck of a bear's teeth must feel
when the salmon is caught.

The moment is frozen, indifferent
and so alive.

I didn't see this but can still hear the splash.

Glaciers calve. I did see one do this.
It was more sound than show.
A gunshot with nobody killed.

I remember gulping real cold, the unsullied freshness
blessing my lungs, but, like the bear, indifferent.
(I would later develop bronchitis.)

Poems for the Camel

Still, I could give my eyes to the stinging brightness,
my heart to an uncluttered country, my intellect
to blankness. Yet we returned to the dampness,
came home to the melted ground
where our lives had rooted.

Here the loneliness is regular, and death
something scheduled for the future.
Soft sounds lull us, the night filled
with familiar noise, the kitchen tap dripping,
a car door opening or closing.

There the wind howls. Chilling. Ungovernable. A bear.
Here we speak the language of machines,
and my refrigerator has an ice maker.
It's attached to a copper coil.
Makes ice cubes like babies.
They clink when they fall.
Mini glaciers.

Boats with Wings and Pajamas with Feet

The best boats look like fish, I'd tell them
as we drew and colored in
the fantastic fins.

Boats with wings are better, this from the younger.
Let's color this one red, chimed in the older.

The thrumming of oar-like propellers flew us up to bed.
The whoosh-whoosh sound on the stairs
as they climbed in their pajamas with feet
is something I like to remember.

Spider-like, I spun tales over their sleepy eyes.
Tonight I wonder, do they still dream of dragons?

Papa, what is death?
Something far away,
I said.

Poems for the Camel

There is no mercy. Fathers and sons grow old.
A heart's leaky valve
and what was far
is close,

the night a giant ear listening

to slow gurgles
deep in the chest,

each labored breath
the measured pace
of a nightmare beast
trapped in a cage.

Long ago, my life was a poem
I sometimes remember.

It's About Someone Lost

It's a relief, this new forgetfulness,
the letting go a pleasure.

How I love to drift,
have my coffee
where I can sit,
and watch the light
come through the lattice.

A simple thing, light
on a tiled floor.

It changes with the calendar.
I can see spring now
and the shift to summer:
a calligraphy I internalize,
my thought a rough brush,
a donkey's tail inked
in the red bean of my brain.

Is there a world outside of me?

I remember once
you kissed the rain off my face.

Now Playing on the Home Box Office in our House

Channel 901

I am a dead factory. My switches off. My levers stuck.
Iced over, the rivers that bring the boats
that feed me are bottled up,
time frozen, the weeks piling,
their unclaimed cargo sitting on the mind's dock
while the heart following cold contracts
weighs me
and finds me lacking,
its monstrous covenants
a silent looming geography.

Wind. Storms. Cold.

The future, endless and demanding,
stretches into the distance,
a treeless, godless tundra.

The camera pans, fanning out in a long panoramic shot.

How will I survive?

Oh please! Another boring documentary.
Stop moaning and change the channel.
The remote is on your side of the bed.

Channel 680

I was born with horns. Two small nubs.

As I grew older, my nature revealed itself.

To my father's horror, I looked like a goat.
The soft pink skin on my face was at odds
with my body's hairy pelt
in a way that made people look away
when my mother wheeled my stroller
down the block.

When I began to talk, I alternated
between words and bleats.

And my feet! It was hard to find shoes
that fit comfortably over my hooves.

Needless to say, I tottered.

This greatly amused my classmates
which lead to schoolyard fights which I won
because I knew how to lower my head,
charge, and butt.

Soon, I discovered the opposite sex and…,

*You know I don't like Science Fiction. And besides,
you've seen* The Goat That Devoured Cleveland *twice.
Change the channel. PLEASE!*

Channel 907

I tell her I still believe that there is a Father,
someone who holds and sifts the sky
sorting the dark from the light,

and who watches over
the souls of all,
who, like us,
are falling.

I tell her we have passed this way before,
our hearts old boats
now beached on the shore.

Time has judged us fairly, found us good.

Soon we'll return to the earth, become its honey,
our wandering sea mouths filled again with dirt.

We will be warm not cold.
The weather of our best years
will roll over the hills
and we'll be born again, two trees
far from our graves.

A hundred years from now,
our great-grandchildren will play
in the park where we live,

their summers spent in laughter
and holy hell.

Under our shade, they too will grow old.

And we, not remembering all that we were,
will watch and wonder why
it all seems so odd,
but familiar.

That movie was sweet.
It felt good, she says
nestling into my shoulder.

Now close the TV. It's late.

ACKNOWLEDGEMENTS

Grateful acknowledgement is made to the following publications in which these poems (some in earlier versions) previously appeared:

The Brownstone's Poet's Anthology (2013): "About the Stove"

City Lit Rag (2012): "It's About Someone Lost"

Icon (2016): "Tintype of Men and a Boy Drinking and smoking Cigars" and "St. Bonaventure's— graveyard and chapel"

Journal of New Jersey Poets (2012): "Suzhou, China"

Meta-Land – Poets of the Palisades II (2016): "Saint Anne de Beaupre"

Narratives Northeast (2012): "After the Long Sigh of the Violins Wound You Beyond Repair"

Narratives Northeast (2014): "Forest Voices"

NinaAlvarez.Net Poem of the Month (November 2017): "Europa"

Passager Poetry Contest Issue (2017): "Boats with Wings and Pajamas with Feet"

Pidgeonholes (May 2017): "Sprout"

The Rutherford Red Wheelbarrow # 4 (2011): "By the Banks of the Nile"

The Rutherford Red Wheelbarrow # 5 (2012): "7 Days Without Dates"

The Rutherford Red Wheelbarrow # 7 (2014): "Grandparents"

The Rutherford Red Wheelbarrow # 8 (2015): "The Eye After Death"

The Rutherford Red Wheelbarrow # 9 (2016): "Home From Alaska"

The Rutherford Red Wheelbarrow # 10 (2017): "Her Cat n the Window Blue with Rain"

The William and Mary Review (2011): "Shakespeare's Moths"

The Unorean (January 2016): "Dead Toes"

The Unorean (April 2016): "Home from Alaska"

Winning Writers (2010): "Cape May, NJ: Memories of an Old House" and "Shakespeare's Moths"

Awards:

Tom Howard Contest for Poetry in All Styles and Genres (Winning Writers, 2010): "Cape May, NJ: Memories of an Old House"- Most Highly Commended and "Shakespeare's Moths" - Most Highly Commended

NinaAlvarez.Net Poem of the Month Contest (November 2017): "Europa"

Also:

In earlier versions, the following poems appeared in Shakespeare's Moths, a privately published collection, (2012): "7 Days Without Dates," "By the Banks of the Nile," "Cape May, NJ: Memories of an Old House," "Melville," and "Shakespeare's Moths."

ABOUT THE AUTHOR

John Barrale's poems and flash fiction have been published in numerous online and print publications. Most recently, his work has appeared in *Unrorean, East Meets West—American Writers Review, Icon, Narrative Northeast, Pidgeonholes, Passager, Sensations Magazine, Molotov Cocktail,* and the NinaAlvarez.net + Cosmographia Books "Poem of the Month."

Along with five other "Gang of Five" members, John hosts and curates a monthly poetry reading series called "The Red Wheelbarrow" at The William Carlos Williams Center in Rutherford, NJ.

In 2012, John joined the volunteer staff of "The Rutherford Red Wheel Barrow" poetry anthologies as one of its two managing editors. He is also managing editor of "The Red Wheelbarrow Poem of the Week" anthologies.

John was born in New York City in 1949, and attended C.U.N.Y community colleges earning a B.A. in English Literature graduating in 1971. Since 1978 John has lived in New Jersey and is currently working hard at being retired, spending most of his tome time writing, reading, and hiking in the U.S. and Canadian national parks.

aviès. pinx.

7ᵉᵐᵉ Ordre

RUMINANTS

Chameau à une bosse ou

Annea

NS OS MARSUPIAUX (Is. G. St Hil.)

adaire (Camelus Dromedarius, L.) 1/24 de grandeur natur.